Can I Go?

by Mary Roberts   illustrated by Ana Martin Larranaga

Harcourt

SCHOOL PUBLISHERS

Requests for permission to make copies of any part of the work should be addressed to School Permissions and Copyrights, Harcourt, Inc., 6277 Sea Harbor Drive, Orlando, Florida 32887-6777. Fax: 407-345-2418.

HARCOURT and the Harcourt Logo are trademarks of Harcourt, Inc., registered in the United States of America and/or other jurisdictions. Printed in China

ISBN 10 0-15-364047-2
ISBN 13 978-0-15-364047-6

6 7 8 9 10   0940   17 16 15 14 13 12 11 10 09

Ordering Options
ISBN 10 0-15-364148-7
ISBN 13 3 978-0-15-364148-0

I am Nat.

Can I go to school?

I can go.

I am Pam.

Can I go to school?

I can go.

 I am at school.

Can I Go?

Word Count: 29

High-Frequency Words	Decodable Words	
go	am	I
to	at	Nat
	can	Pam